The Chinese Christian Citizen

In Contemporary China

Dr. Kenneth G. Arndt

The Chinese Christian Citizen in Contemporary China

May 2012 published by Chinese Christian Theological Association
874 Beacon Street, Boston, Massachusetts, 02215- 3101USA
www.CCTA2009.org
ISBN-13: 978-1477544877   ISBN-10: 1477544879
Printed in the United States of America

The Chinese Christian Citizen in Contemporary China

A Paper Presented at the Chinese Christian Theological
Association Conference in Summer 2010

Dr. Kenneth G. Arndt

kgarndt@gmail.com

Table of Contents

Preface

I heartily beg that what I have here done may be read with candor; and that the defects I have been guilty of upon this subject may be not so much reprehended as kindly supplied, and investigated by new endeavors of my readers.

- Isaac Newton, Preface to the *Principia*, 1686.

It must be stated that it would be presumptuous for a citizen of a Western country to attempt, based upon the Western culture, experience, and thinking, to teach Chinese Christians, even if they are fellow believers, the path for them to take in creating a paradigm for Christian citizenship. That task is for Chinese Christians to define for themselves. All Christians in every age and country must respond to the unique cultural and political situation into which they are born. That response for Christians has always rested on their understanding of what the Scriptures teach about social virtue and responsibility toward God and the State.

The defining principles that form the foundation of a Christian citizen's response to the leadership and laws of his country are to be determined by what the Creator God has said governs these relationships. [1] These principles have been shown to be applicable to various social and political environments across recorded history. That is to say that Christians faithful to the Word of God can be virtuous citizens of many if not all forms of human government. That is not to say that they always have been faithful to their principles or successful in their implementation. [2] As Martin Luther (1483-1586) expressed the state of Christians while alive on the earth, they are at the same time declared holy before God and yet still prone to sin.

As the hand cannot be properly understood without the context of the entire body, so Christians believe that man cannot be properly understood without reference to God and what he has revealed about himself in the Bible. Knowledge of the greatest context is the greatest knowledge. While Christians seek knowledge of this world

---

[1] The most important question ever asked of mankind is that ancient question "Did God actually say. . ." Genesis 3:1. The failure to properly answer that question has devastating consequences. All Scripture references are from the English Standard Version unless otherwise noted.

[2] Stanley J. Grenz, "Beyond Foundationalism: Is a Nonfoundationalist Evangelical Theology Possible?" *Christian Scholar's Review* XXX:1 (Fall 2000). p77. "The theologian's task, then, is not to work from an interpretive framework to a theological construct. Instead, the theological enterprise consists in setting forth in a systematic manner a properly Christian interpretative framework as informed by the Bible for the sake of the mission of the Church in the contemporary context."

they do not revere it as the highest knowledge by which to derive meaning for life. Christians see that there can be a danger in seeking only knowledge of this world here on earth:

> Every man naturally desires knowledge, but what good is knowledge without fear of God? Indeed a humble rustic who serves God is better than a proud intellectual who neglects his soul to study the course of the stars.
>
> If I knew all things in the world and had not charity, what would it profit me before God Who will judge me by my deeds?
>
> Shun too great a desire for knowledge, for in it there is much fretting and delusion. Intellectuals like to appear learned and to be called wise. Yet there are many things the knowledge of which does little or no good to the soul, and he who concerns himself about other things than those which lead to salvation is very unwise.
>
> Many words do not satisfy the soul; but a good life eases the mind and a clean conscience inspires great trust in God.
>
> The more you know and the better you understand, the more severely will you be judged, unless your life is also the more holy.[3]

---

[3] The quotations cited above are from Thomas A. Kempis, *The Imitation of Christ*, trans. by Aloysius Croft and Harold Bolton, (Mineola, NY: Dover Publications, Inc, 2003). p.2. First published anonymously in 1418 it is a

It is necessary both that Christians understand the foundations of their faith and the citizenship that flows from that knowledge, and that the government and culture Christians live in understand the mindset of Christians which guides their behavior. Each side must have a frame of reference large enough in order to make sense of how to approach each other. Looking at a situation that carries the potential for miscommunication and resistance without each side attempting to understand the other does not produce harmony in any society. Christians must explain themselves to their respective cultures; governments, to rule wisely, should listen.

Cultures, ruled over by governments, are nearly always pluralistic in nature. There are many contending viewpoints: religious, social, political, economic, etc. Each mindset seeks to interpret reality based upon certain foundational assumptions about man's condition on this earth and what to do about it. What is to be done to give us a harmonious and just society? Where is "salvation" from the problems of our finite lives to be found? One

---

Christian classic. Modern scholarship ascribes it to two or three men, members of the Brethren of the Common Life, who were priests in the Netherlands in the late fourteenth century. Thomas Hemerken of Kempen (Thomas A Kempis) is thought to have created the work from their spiritual diary. Interestingly, there is in a Buddhist Temple complex in Beijing a series of upright stone memorials to those men in several dynasties who passed the Imperial exams. Their names are often worn away by time and the weather so that their identities are lost. Where are these men now, and what was the meaning of their lives?

scholar attempting to clarify the problems states:

> If salvation is the experience of 'illumination,' then perhaps Buddha 'saves.' If salvation is 'the experience of union with the cosmic All' then perhaps Hinduism 'saves.' If salvation is being faithful to one's ancestors,' then perhaps Shintoism 'saves.' If salvation is 'being freed from the oppression of the bourgeoisie,' then perhaps Marxism 'saves.'
>
> If salvation is 'material well-being,' then perhaps Capitalism 'saves.' 'If salvation means 'feeling good,' then perhaps there is salvation not only outside of Christ but outside of religion in general.[4]

The author, a Christian scholar, goes on to say that if the basic problem of mankind is none of the above but what the Bible calls sin (rebellion against Heaven) resulting in a lack of justice among men in relationships with each other and the anger of God requiring liberation from the power of sin and death, then only Jesus saves.

Utopian visions of every kind have been put forward by the mind of man in order to fulfill the desires of individuals and groups. But is seems that all utopian visions, no matter how powerful in the minds of men to inspire, shipwreck on the failure to change human nature

---

[4] Carl F. Braaten, "The Uniqueness and Universality of Jesus Christ," in *Mission Trends*, No.5, pp.82-83.

however much they proclaim they can or how hard they try and force the change to build a better man. Che Guevara made the statement about the Cuban revolution; "If this revolution is not aimed at changing people, then I am not interested."[5]

The type of change he advocated was not love, but hatred:

> Hatred is a factor in the struggle, unending hatred of the enemy, which takes the individual beyond his natural limitations and transforms him into an effective, violent, selective and cold mechanism of death. That's how our soldiers must be. A people without hatred cannot win against our brutal enemy.[6]

The Christian citizen takes another path toward a just and harmonious society. He takes the path of service and love, impacting his culture according to the teachings of God's revelation in the Bible. Not in a perfect way and never ending in perfection by man's efforts in this life.

---

[5] This quote was carved into a hospital wall in Cuba and noted by Brother Andrew in his book, *The Calling: A Challenge to Walk the Narrow Road*, (Grand Rapids, MI: Fleming H. Revell,2002), p.171.

[6] Ibid, p.171. It has ever been the dream of political thinkers to be able to change human nature and build a utopian brave new world. "The word UTOPIA stands in common usage for the ultimate in human folly or human hope – vain dreams of perfection in a Never-Never Land or rational efforts to remake man's environment and his institutions and even his own erring nature, so as to enrich the possibilities of the common life." Quoted from: Lewis Mumford, *The Story of Utopias*, (NY: The Viking Press, 1962), p.1.

But Christians striving to live virtuous lives provide a means to hold a harmonious society together by being honest, telling the truth, and helping their neighbors. When most forms of government are enthralled by the charisma of power, Christians are enthralled by the charisma of grace (unmerited favor of God) and are inspired and empowered by God to share His love.

The Christian vision is not one of man-made utopianism seeking to create a Heaven on earth where God's law rules in all things through human effort. The prayer Jesus taught Christians to pray, "May your will be done on earth as it is in Heaven,"[7] asks God to bring it about. It will happen when and how God rules, not as the result of human effort or creation of a Christian utopian political or economic movement.

Postmodern[8] or Post-Enlightenment[9] Western society

---

[7] Matthew 6:10

[8] The term "postmodernism" has been defined and used in many ways. C. Stephen Evens, *The Pocket Dictionary of Apologetics & Philosophy of Religion* (Downers Grove, IL: InterVarsity Press, 2002), describes it as follows: "The term is used to designate a loosely connected set of trends and perspectives in various cultural and academic fields that have in common only a perceived opposition to modernity. In philosophy, postmodernism is characterized by a suspicion of "metanarratives," an emphasis on the uncertain character of human knowing, and a tendency to analyze various intellectual claims, including, Enlightenment claims about the universal character of reason and science, in a suspicious way as a mask for oppression and domination."

[9] Immanuel Kant (1724-1804) in the famous opening to his "An Answer to the Question: What Is Enlightenment?" defined it as:

is in a crisis of confidence in the power of reason to find a foundational worldview:

> The Enlightenment's failure to provide a foundation for ethics and Society has left us with no way to counter the widespread attitude that values are mere expressions of personal preferences. This is in effect to deny the reality of good and evil.[10]

This has led to a secular mentality of pluralism and relativism. Christianity has been abandoned as a valid intellectual pursuit to solve man's problem of alienation.[11]

Enlightenment is man's release from his self incurred tutelage. Tutelage is man's inability to make use of his understanding without direction from another. Self incurred is this tutelage when its cause lies not in lack of reason but in lack of resolution and courage to use it without direction from another. *Sapere aude*,

"Have courage to use your own reason!" – that is the motto of the Enlightenment. Kant wanted to rescue reason and science from Hume's extreme skepticism and keep the Enlightenment project moving forward. He hoped for a universal scientific knowledge based upon our experiences as interpreted by our minds.

[10] Diogenes Allen, *Christian Belief in a Postmodern World*, (Louisville, KY: Westminster/John Knox Press, 1989), p.18.

[11] See especially, Eric and Mary Josephson, eds., *Man Alone: Alienation in Modern Society*, (NY: Dell Publishing, 1962). ". . . Western man feels deeply troubled as he faces the immense gulf between his finest achievements of hand and brain, and his own sorry ineptitude at coping with them; between his truly awe-inspiring accomplishments and the utter failure of his imagination to encompass them and give them meaning. Powerless in the face of modern mechanical and social forces, we have reached a point of history where knowledge and tools intended originally to serve man now threaten to destroy him." p.9.

The failure of the Enlightenment vision of the power of reason and knowledge to order our lives and societies has led to a plurality of worldviews striving for position in the minds of men.

Post-Enlightenment thinking in both philosophy and science has challenged the abandonment of religion in general and Christianity in particular as the assumptions of the Enlightenment about man and reality have been reexamined:

> Many people both in the West and among the Western-educated in Asia and Africa still do not know of the developments in science and philosophy which render those assumptions untenable. Western culture at large is still in the process of moving away from those assumptions. As we continue to do so, the fact that there is a plurality of worldviews and religions will continue to drive some people toward relativism. But if we can exhibit the intellectual strength of Christianity, we can render a service both to those who are still captives of the assumptions of the Enlightenment and think that belief in God as Creator and Redeemer in Christ is impossible for an educated mind and to those who are free of those assumptions but are now adrift. [12]

---

[12] Diogenes Allen, *Christian Belief in a Postmodern World*, pp.9-10.

Introduction

This paper will attempt to put forward suggestions for consideration of virtuous Christian citizenship in the contemporary Chinese state as it develops into the 21st century. It is a defense of particularly Christian citizenship as opposed to a model for all religions and opposed to a philosophical materialistic worldview. It seeks to portray the teachings of Christianity as both reasonable and beneficial to a given society. Other citizenship models at work in modern China also define and seek to implement a virtuous citizenship. While references to the current political/social situation in China, Confucianism, Daoism, and Buddhism and Islam are made in an attempt to suggest points of contact, these comments are not the focus of this paper and would require separate and careful study. But a dialog along these lines between competing models of virtuous citizenship could produce a better mutual understanding, respect, and just proportion between differing world views, and promote social peace and progress.

Attempts to maintain a single vision of citizenship in so large and diverse a country as China have clearly failed and remain an unrealistic goal.Therefore, accommodations must be sought between contending value sets for the sake of social peace and modern development. A core set of values around societal relationships should be identified and utilized in order to maintain forward economic progress and a peaceful transition into the 21st century.

Much of the thinking of world leaders relies upon social theory informed by what are believed to be facts about man and nature supported by logic and science. As we will see there is not agreement on just what constitutes a fact and the proper definition of man. All social theories are based upon certain assumptions about reality used as a foundation from which to build society and culture. These can be religious or materialistic, but none are apparently absolutely certain or proven always correct:

> Facts cannot be proved by presumptions, yet it is remarkable that in cases where nothing stronger than presumption was even professed, scientific men have sometimes acted as if they thought this kind of argument, taken by itself decisive of a fact which was in debate.[13]

On the basis of a materialistic and relativistic philosophical worldview, the idea of universally valid ethical principles and moral values "social reformers can have appeal only to social consensus, a most fragile entity.

---

[13] John Henry Newman, *An Essay in Aid of a Grammar of Assent*, (Garden City, NY: Doubleday, 1955), pp.298-99.

Being the target of increasingly skillful manipulations, that consensus is the process of fragmenting, with anarchy waiting in the wings."[14]

In China the growing disparity of economic opportunity and fulfilled expectations between the huge rural population and the much smaller urban population along the developing coastal regions puts a growing strain upon the rule of the central government.

The pressures of a growing population, their food, potable water, and the jobs needed to support them coupled with the impact of ecological pollution, high demand for resources and infrastructure pose immense problems and pressures upon core values of what it means to be a virtuous citizen in contemporary China.

The Chinese government is very aware of the unrest, especially in the countryside but also in urban settings that is constantly being set off by injustices perceived in the midst of rapid development and economic success. These incidents of unrest, despite the attempts of the government to limit their impact by limiting information about them, are becoming well known in China and in the wider world through the growing use in China of the Internet. It

---

[14] Stanley L. Jaki, *The Only Chaos and Other Essays*, (Lanham, MD: University Press of America, 1990), "Extra-Terrestrials and Scientific Progress," p.101. Dr. Jaki holds doctorates in theology and physics and has written more than thirty books. His books are always rewarding to read.

remains to be seen if all the holes in the Great Internet Firewall can be plugged to the satisfaction of those in power. Centralized authorities in all political systems seem to have problems with the free flow of information among their citizens.

The temptation among governments is that the control of the flow of information is an efficient means to control and mold public opinion. This is often harder than it looks as technology develops and those trained in and developing the technology are the ones who want access to information.[15]

---

[15] The press played a powerful role in the French Revolution. Censorship, repression, and suspension of freedom of the press was tried without complete success at various times against the early revolutionaries in Europe in the nineteenth century. The revolutionaries in France and Belgium of 1830 looked forward to

". . . the day when every citizen shall be able to have a press in his home, just as he has the right to pen and paper." Cited in James H. Billington, Fire *in the Minds of Men: Origins of the Revolutionary Faith*, (New Brunswick, NJ: Transaction Press, 2007), p.310. See his chapter, "The Magic Medium: Journalism." Today we have the Internet and it is still possible to censor.

I. Religious/Human Rights Conditions in Contemporary China: Two Points of View

The Chinese state wishes to be perceived by the world as living up to the statements in its founding documents[16] and laws regarding religious freedoms and to be in line with the United Nations Charter in these areas. It takes great exception to statements made otherwise for example, the 2006 United States State Department report that China is among the world's nations that repress religious expression and human rights:[17]

> Although the constitution asserts that 'the state respects and preserves human rights,' the

---

[16] *Constitution of the People's Republic of China,* Adapted 12/4/1982, Article 36:

"Citizens of the People's Republic of China enjoy freedom of religious belief. No organ, public organization or individual may compel citizens to believe in, or not to believe in, a religion; nor may they discriminate against citizens who believe in, or do not believe in, any religion. The state protects normal religious activities." Of course that last sentence is open to state interpretation.

[17] See the *"Freedom of Religious Belief in China"* report issued by the Information Office of the State Council of the People's Republic of China, October, 1997, Beijing.
www.chineseculture.about.com/library/china/whitepaper/blsreligion.htm
Accessed 6/10/07. It strongly supports the claim of religious freedoms in China supported by the rule of law.

government's human rights record remained poor, and in certain areas deteriorated. The government tightened restrictions on freedom of speech and the press, including stricter control and censorship of the Internet. Nongovernmental organizations (NGOs), both local and international, continued to face increased scrutiny and restrictions. Individuals and groups, especially those considered politically sensitive, continued to face tight restrictions on their freedom to assemble; their freedom to practice religion, including strengthened enforcement of religious affairs regulations implemented in 2005; and their freedom to travel.[18]

China of course can and does point to the record on human rights of the United States. In response to the 2005 US State Department report on China's human rights record, the State Council, China's cabinet, denounced in turn this then latest report from America:

As in previous years, the state department pointed the finger at human rights situations in more than 190 countries and regions, including China, but kept silent on the serious violations of human rights in the US. To help people realize the true features of this self-styled 'guardian of human rights, it is necessary to probe into the human rights abuses in the United States in

---

[18] Quoted from the "US Department of State Country Reports on Human Rights Practice 2006" released by the Bureau of Democracy, Human Rights, and Labor, March 6, 2007.

2005.[19]

This back and forth tit for tat "dialog" has not proven to be helpful. A model for a vital worthwhile Christian citizen living out his faith in word and deed can be offered as necessary and helpful to the broader state goals of a peaceful and productive society. Condemnation without proof of offense and offer of a counter solution to problems can sometimes be perceived only as an attack and the casting of blame. Christians do indeed speak of sin, their own as well as the sin of others, but the Gospel, the "Good News" is that there is a better way of social relationships provided by God. Christians offer a virtuous model of citizenship that is beneficial to the stability of the state rather than being a threat to the state.

It is important to understand that many in the government of China view religion as a potential destabilizing force in society especially perhaps among the vast peasant population. They well remember the role of religion in the events leading to the communist collapse in Eastern Europe. [20] They also clearly understand the

---

[19] Quoted at
www.int.iol.co.za/index.php?set_id=1&click_id=3&art_id=qw114187950134
6R131 Accessed 5/23/07. This response mentions gun-related crimes, police abuse, and the US poverty level as well as American troop abuses at Abu Graib prison in Iraq and at Guantanamo Bay in Cuba.

[20] See the report of Ron Argue on a visit and meetings with Chinese authorities, including President Jiang Zemin.
www.religiousfreedom.com/conference/Dc/argue.htm. Accessed 5/15/07.

growth of religion in China [21] and claim, in public statements, to understand that its impact upon society can be beneficial. [22] However too often Christians, or those who take the name of Christian, do not follow the teachings of Jesus to altruistically work for the betterment of society and their fellow man. Christians bring shame upon the name of Jesus when they lie and cheat and steal. [23]

---

[21] See especially the official report, English edition on-line, of *China Daily*, "Religious Believers Thrice the Estimate. " www.chinadaily.com.cn/china/2007-02/07/content_802994.htm   Accessed 6/10/07.

The article tells of many new young people both from rural and developed areas along the coasts turning to religious faith of all kinds. It should be noted that these young people and older people also grew up under communist teachings. Communist Russia saw the same phenomenon as "grandmothers' and youths filled the churches in the 1970s and 1980s. The religious survey referenced in this article was first published in the Chinese-language Oriental Outlook magazine.

[22] The *China Daily* article "Religious Believers Thrice the Estimate" quotes Professor Liu Zhongyu of the Shanghai-based East China Normal University as saying, "For example, religious beliefs have helped cut down crime to a large extent."

[23] A good example of a bad Christian example of how to live in society is how in the west American Christians often treated the native peoples. Certainly there were some bad and good native people just as not all those who claimed to be Christian were either good or bad. But those who do not live out the precepts of Christian love tend to color all Christians in the minds of non-Christians. Red Jacket (1750-1830), a Seneca chief had this to say about the Christians he met:

Go, then, and teach the whites. Select, for example, the people of Buffalo. We will be spectators, and remain silent. Improve their morals and refine their habits – make them less disposed to cheat Indians. Make the whites generally less inclined to make Indians drunk, and to take from them

Ron Argue quotes President Jiang Zemin in a meeting with Christians:

> Jiang said he believed the main message of the Bible was "to purify man's soul as a lofty work." He observed that the reality of religious practice has not always fulfilled the founder's faith or ideals. Foreign powers, he said, had bullied China during the 19th century, and many improper acts were carried out in the name of religion. Nevertheless, he recognized that religion can play a positive role in China and showed interest in expanding religious activities there.

An interesting part of our discussion centered on the fact that the best universities and hospitals in China were founded by Western missionary groups. He acknowledged that. In fact, he spoke of being treated as a youth in a hospital in Shanghai that was an evangelical missionary hospital. "Differences can be gradually narrowed and common ground broadened," he said. President Jiang said that he and the Chinese government would carefully consider the proposals and concerns raised by our delegation.[24]

---

their lands. Let us know the tree by the blossoms and the blossoms by the fruit. When this shall be made clear to our minds we may be more willing to listen to you. Quoted in: Author Caswell Parker, *Red Jacket: Seneca Chief*, (Lincoln and London: University of Nebraska Press, 1998), p. xvii.

[24] See the on-line Ron Argue referenced site for the full report on his dialog with various government officials. Some of them admitted to vastly expanded

It would be helpful to understand the definition of terms used when in dialog with others with whom we may not agree. Does "freedom of religion" really mean the same thing to those in the American State Department and those in the Chinese Cabinet? Would we understand better the differences if it were pointed out that to the Chinese government "freedom of religion" means freedom to worship but not necessarily freedom to do so in as public a manner as in the West or as part of the educational and service sectors of the society?

II. Some Models of Citizenship Competing in China Today

The purpose of briefly looking at other than a Christian model of citizenship is not to expound upon their history and practice but to point out suggestions for points of contact and dialog while considering the implications of a uniquely Christian model. It should be obvious to the observer of the historical and current results of the Christian attempt to define relationships with neighbors and states that these attempts have taken many forms with varied success. There appears not to be a "one size fits all" cross-cultural Christian answer. The Apostles and the early Church Fathers have left us a record of decisions and

numbers of Christians over the "official" estimate.

suggestions for social relationships. The issue is to begin from basic Scriptural principles and achieve a model for our particular time and culture.

It is true that the Scripture clearly states that our primary spiritual citizenship as Christians is in heaven. "So then you are no longer strangers and aliens, but you are fellow citizens with the saints and members of the household of God."[25] "But our citizenship is in heaven and we await a Savior, the Lord Jesus Christ."[26] This does not mean that Christians ignore citizenship in this world, rather it means that because of the hope of an eternally harmonious life to come we can face this life with courage and a sense of just proportion. This is seen perhaps most clearly in St. Augustine's *City of God* in which he points out that Christians need to recognize how being a member of the heavenly city also impacts our citizenship in earthly cities in this life:

> This heavenly city, then, while on its pilgrimage on earth, calls out its citizens from every nation, and gathers a society of travelers in every linguistic community. It is not concerned what differences there may be in those morals, laws, or institutions by which earthly peace is achieved and preserved. These do not have to be abolished

---

[25] Ephesians 2:19

[26] Philippians 3:20

> or destroyed; no, though different traditions prevail in different peoples, they may be protected and observed insofar as they serve the one end of earthly peace, provided they do not impede the religion which teaches the worship of the one supreme and true God.[27]

We see here in this statement both the value of Christian citizenship to any nation and the limits of Christian citizenship. Chinese Christians, like any citizens, simply want the rights of religious freedom as expressed in the Chinese Constitution and to live in peace and contribute to the peace of the nation. Left in peace they will be a foundation, a pillar contributing to the moral fabric of both their neighbors and the state. Of course not every Christian always lives up to such a high standard of Christian core values and so should also, as citizens of the nation, be subject to the just laws of the nation. This is true as we always keep in mind the question of authority. Christianity, as well as Chinese tradition, recognizes the rule of Heaven in the affairs of men and their governments when considering the ordering of a just society.

Christians see themselves as members of the Kingdom of Heaven which is an eternal ordering of being

---

[27] Augustine, *The City of God*, Book 19:16, quoted in Oliver O'Donovan and Joan Lockwood O'Donovan, eds., *From Irenaeus to Grotius: A Sourcebook in Christian Political Thought,* (Grand Rapids, MI: Wm B. Eerdmans Publishing Company, 1999), p.160. This book is indeed an interesting and helpful work on Christian political insight and thought.

established for us "from the foundation of the world." (Matthew 25: 34). It is not some external order in this life such as the state or even the family, but it speaks to our heart's longing for more than all the pleasures of this life so soon to end. The Gospel of Jesus Christ, the good news, is the "more" of life that our souls require. It is as S. L. Frank (1877-1950) expresses it:

> The good news has another and an immeasurably greater significance for us, contemporary people, who have lost our faith and are conscious of ourselves as defenseless orphans, abandoned in an alien, hostile world. The tragic nature of our contemporary metaphysical feeling based on unfaith consists in the consciousness of our utter abandonedness, in the consciousness that we are hanging over an abyss into which we are doomed to fall or that we are the playthings of indifferent forces of nature (including blind human passions and urges). With regard to this life-feeling, the good news of the kingdom as the desired eternal homeland or ground of man's being is an absolute revolution, which replaces fear and despair with the wholly apposite joyful feeling of the complete assuredness and stability of our being.[28]

We shall now turn to a Western political ideal of

---

[28] S. L. Frank, *The Light Shineth in Darkness: An Essay in Christian Ethics and Social Philosophy*, (Ohio University Press, 1989), p.60. S. L. Frank was a Russian thinker who lived through the struggles of the Russian Revolution and what followed. Today he is hardly known, but his books are worth reading.

proper citizenship imported into China by atheists who rejected any higher authority than man himself. The story starts perhaps with Auguste Comte who founded his theory of positivist science and social theory on the physics of his day.[29] As Jaki comments:

> Karl Marx referred to the laws of physics in the Preface of *Das Kapital* and claimed that the laws of history, as he set them forth, were as exact and definitive as those of mechanistic physics. Darwin himself wished nothing more than to know the chemical mechanism underlying the process of evolution.[30]

III. The Party-State Citizen in China

Under the rule of the Communist Party the role of the citizen was envisioned as the new socialist man who would work hard and selflessly for the good of all. Perhaps the most famous slogan of Chairman Mao was "Serve the People." While many, especially idealistic youth, did sacrifice themselves for the values of the revolution the country could not seem to eliminate or

---

[29] It is a constant mistake made even by some thinkers today to take the current state of knowledge in a given field for the final state. Karl Marx and Charles Darwin fell into this same trap.

[30] Quoted in, Stanley L. Jaki, *The Only Chaos and Other Essays*, "Physics or Physicalism: A Cultural Dilemma," p.163.

control corruption or inflation in the economic or social spheres. This was human nature vs. idealism and human nature seems to have won out. With the passing of Chairman Mao and new leadership (Deng) a new slogan gained popularity, "It's glorious to be rich." This may not always imply service.

The awakening of China and its explosion onto center stage in the 21st century with its enormous economic growth has caused an almost exponential pace of change and a search for core values. This is an open debate with China. For example *China Daily* ran an editorial entitled "Modern China Needs Some Old Thinking" in which the author, You Nuo suggests his readers look to traditional wisdom (Confucian) for moral values needed for any society to progress:

> No society can afford to build an economy without a moral foundation. It is hard to imagine millions of people selling and buying from each other every day without sharing a basic, although often tacit, agreement of how a good business person should behave. . . . Yet a moral system does offer immense help to an economy, and more so to a transitional economy. When the rule of law is weak, and many rules that were made in the era of the planned economy are obsolete, a return to traditional teachings is a natural choice

for many people.[31]

The state wants economic growth but that means less central planning and some economic liberalization and the relinquishment of a degree of social control. But while laws and more freedom in the markets can lead to growth there needs to be a moral cement to generate social habits that can hold society together. Religion is often called upon to respond to this need.[32]

IV. Historical Attempts at Stability – Rome

The desire to find religious, political, or philosophical

---

[31] You Nuo, *China Daily* English version on-line, 7/31/06.
www.chinadaily.com.cn/opinion2006-07/31/content_654179.htm

In 1990 China adopted an administration litigation law under which citizens have the right to make complaints or charges against any state organ if it has violated the law. In 1997 China adopted a revised criminal procedures law which specifies that a suspect cannot be held incommunicado for more than seven days. As in any country, including the United States, the distance between the law and its actual application is often greater than hoped for. Loopholes exist. When the Party took up the slogan "The rule of Law" (*yi fa zhi gao*) its application has not always been what Westerners might have concluded it meant. See "The Rule of Law" in Jasper Becker, *The Chinese*. (NY: The Free Press, 2000), pp.314-340.

[32] www.chinaview.cn 12-07-2005 reports the funding by Peking University and the Ministry of Education of an effort to compile the first ever comprehensive collection of Confucian literature. It will take scholars 16 years to complete. Over 300 scholars from 25 countries are taking part. It is expected to comprise at least 5000 books. Attempts at collecting the cannons of Buddhism and Daoism have been compiled in the past. The goal is to make available to the world the benefit of Confucian insights and teaching.

roots upon which to rebuild society is an ancient one. In the writings of Sallust (86-35B.C.) we find him describing the loss of purpose among the people of Rome after the great war with Carthage has been won. The war gave the people a vision to unite them but there was a great decline in values after the threat of war was removed. It seems that the ancient Roman citizens would be right at home in the modern world. This kind of behavior is seen all over the world today as well:

> But when the people were relieved of this fear, the favorite vices of prosperity – license and pride – appeared as a natural consequence. Thus peace and quiet which they had longed for in time of adversity proved, when they obtained it, to be ever more grievous and bitter than the adversity. For the nobles started to use their positions, and the people their liberty, to gratify their selfish passions, every man snatching and seizing what he could for himself.[33]

Paul Johnson the English writer (b. 1923) describes Rome at a later time as it tries to recover its values and traditions:

> Rome itself periodically attempted to recover its virtuous and creative past. Augustus Caesar, while creating an empire on the eve of the Christian period, looked back to the noble spirit

---

[33] Quoted in *The Jugurthine War* (Baltimore, MD: Penguin Classics, 1972), p.82.

of the Republic, and even beyond it to the very origins of the City, to establish moral and cultural continuities, and so legitimize his regime. The court historian Livy resurrected the past in prose, the court epic poet Virgil told the story of Rome's divinely blessed origins in verse.[34]

V. The Present – the West

In the West today there is also a struggle to find a foundation on which to build a vision of an orderly and just society. In the United States the stirring words of the Declaration of Independence no longer has weight in a secular world that no longer looks to the Christian God. "We hold these truths to be self-evident, that all men are created equal and endowed by their Creator with certain unalienable rights." As the French philosopher Jean Paul Sartre (1905-1980) was said to have remarked, "A finite point is without meaning except connected to an infinite reference point." Without a higher power than our own rationality and insight on what do we attempt to build a political structure and call all men to acclaim it as right and just? It is a question of authority. Does political power really come from the finger on the trigger of a gun? This dilemma is portrayed in the arts.

---

[34] Paul Johnson, *The Renaissance: A Short Story*, (London: Phoenix Press, 2000), p.5.

Speaking of Samuel Beckett (1905-1989) the Irish playwright, Valency says:

> Beckett's plays grow progressively shorter, more enigmatic and more inarticulate, until in the end they approximate gestures. One cannot say that after a time words failed him. Few writers of our age have had words so completely at their command. But the need to speak, so strongly evident in Beckett's early works, seems bit by bit to have diminished once he found a hearing. In his mind, the inability to speak and the inability to be silent appear in time to have reached a state of equilibrium.[35]

Becket has become a speaker with nothing to say, a singer with no song, an artist with no subject to paint!

David Cornwell[36] writing spy novels under the name of "John Le Carre" in his novel *Absolute Friends* has a communist revolutionary who has lost faith in his vision say:

> Writing to you at this moment I am ready to give up half of what I believe in exchange for one clarifying vision. To see one great rational truth glowing on the horizon, to go to it regardless of

---

[35] Marurice Valency, *The End of the World: An Introduction to Contemporary Drama* (NY: Oxford University Press, 1980), p.418. See especially, available on YouTube, Beckett's 1.25 second play *Breath.*

[36] Cornwell was a British spy for five years before being betrayed to the Russian KGB.

cost, regardless of what must be left behind, is what I dream of beyond all things.[37]

If we are to build a better world than this, I asked myself, where do we turn, whose actions do we support . . . You know I have the Lutheran curse. Conviction without action has no meaning for me. Yet what is conviction? How do I identify it? How can we know that we should be guided by it? Is it found in the heart, or in the intellect? And what if it is only to be found in the one and not the other? [38]

VI. Religious Citizenship in China

Confucianism has a long history in China and many interpreters. [39] Mencius and Xun Zi developed Confucianism into an ethical and political doctrine. Mencius founded his doctrine on the idea that human nature is basically good and popularized the five relationships concept. Xun Zi did the opposite. He believed that human nature was bad and must be controlled and taught to be good by the use of education

---

[37] John Le Carre, *Absolute Friends* (Boston: Little Brown & Co., 2003), p.126.

[38] Ibid., p.216.

[39] The Six Schools: Han Confucianism, Neo-Confucianism, Contemporary Neo-Confucianism, and also the Korean, Japanese, and Singapore Confucianism schools.

and rituals. Of course since their time Confucianism has be interpreted in many ways – the school of the Neo-Confucians influenced by Zhu Xi combining some Daoist and Buddhist ideas with Confucian ideas. Confucianism has a strong sense of forming a stable and harmonious community. The Confucian system of government was designed, through the use of qualifying examinations to produce men responsible to rule who were upright and learned men of scholarship who would rule with proper judgment.

The Confucian concepts of virtue have counterparts with Christian values. *Ren, Yi, Li, and Zhi,* all can be found in the Christian Scripture in some form. The Confucian practice of delegating the status of women as being subservient to men, largely perhaps from the interpretation of the "Yin" as somewhat negative or the relationship of husband and wife has unfortunately a counterpart of some Christian misinterpretations of Scripture on the status of women.[40] As the education level of women all over the world goes up this kind of thinking will cause many problems for any society which refuses to change. The Christian model is for the woman to be a

---

[40] The Hebrew culture of the 1st century followed Greek cultural practices and placed women at a lower level than men. "Thank you God that you did not make me a woman" was a prayer of Jewish men of that time – similar to a Greek prayer. But Paul, while not allowing women uneducated in the Law to teach men (women were not sent to schools), overthrew that prayer with the clear statement that there is no male or female when standing before God.

"helpmate for man. Christians of virtue are called to show respect for God-appointed authority (I Peter 3: 3), to other members of their own families, the entire Christian community, and those in the greater unbelieving community as well.

Daoism offers a view of reality that mainly stresses nostalgia for a simpler time of origins that were a state of chaotic wholeness sometimes called *hundun*. In that state nothing is lacking and reality is as if it were an uncarved block of stone before the first cut is made:

> Once birth happens – once the stone is cut – however, the world descends into a state of imperfection. Rather than a mythological sin on the part of the first human beings or an ontological separation of God from humanity, the Daoist version of the Fall involves division into parts, the assigning of names, and the leveling of judgments injurious to life.[41]

Some Daoist belief claims contact with higher beings and the individual hope of the Daoist practioner is to become a higher eternal being who is reunited with the

---

[41] Stephen F. Teiser, Quote from *Religions of Asia in Practice: An Anthology*, Edited by Donald S. Lopez, Jr. (Princeton: Princeton University Press, 2002), p.300. He quotes from the *Dao de jing* (The Classic on the Way and Its Power), "The Dao gave birth to the One, the One gave birth to the Two, the Two gave birth to the Three, and the Three gave birth to the Ten Thousand Things." One wonders what caused that first great division of the One? How or why did the Dao "give birth?

"One." Here similar and yet different answers to the meaning and purpose of life as held between Daoism and Christianity. Christianity has a much stronger view of community and therefore citizenship involvement with a modern state. Christians also seek peace and fulfillment even in the midst of suffering, but in relationship to a personal "One."

Buddhism seeks to offer an explanation for suffering in this life that leads to the path of salvation. It defines high moral values as a means to achieve liberation:

> Traditional formulations of Buddhist practice describe a path to salvation that begins with the observance of morality. Lay followers pledged to abstain from the taking of life, stealing, lying, drinking intoxicating beverages, and engaging in sexual relations outside of marriage.[42]

As can be immediately seen, these values agree with Christian virtues. The source is different and the reason for doing them is different but this does formulate a point of contact for dialog and mutual respect. There is also a great difference between Christianity and most other religions of the world and the modern secular state in that the antidote to man's foundational problem of being finite is not power or technique, religious or secular, but security in the love of God:

---

[42] Ibid. p 306. Again, one wonders what caused the need for "salvation?"

What unites most ancient Eastern religious and
modern Western secular humanisms is the quest
for *techniques of power*, techniques that will
confer self-mastery and/or the mastery of the
natural order. The gods of Indian and Chinese
pantheons are essentially personifications of
various forms of power. Devotion and ritual, less
demanding than the rigorous contemplative
techniques of the mystics, has as their goal
freedom from vulnerability, suffering and
contingency. The right formula, the correct
devotional posture, the appropriate prescribed
offering. . . these are the preoccupations of the
traditional devotee. In the modern technocratic
world, finding the right advertising slogan, the
correct management method, or the appropriate
political style have come to dominate the lives of
many men and women. Manipulation of the
'spiritual' realm is now combined with the
manipulation of the human and material realms
in the technocratic spirituality of the New Age.[43]

VII. China and Islam

Islam is often viewed today through the lens of the
struggle against the Western countries. It is seen as having
a rigid religious social structure that allows no or very
little freedom of social relationships. This is far from the

[43] Vinoth Ramachandra, *Gods That Fail: Modern Idolatry and Christian Mission*, (Downers Grove, IL: InterVarsity Press, 1996), p. 211.

truth. Islam has a long history of accommodation to various cultures and interpretations of the *Koran.* The Muslim population of China will not long remain unaffected by this debate within the Islamic world community. In an ever smaller, better educated, internet, globalized world, change and challenges come ever more quickly to all governments.

The world-wide struggle and search for core values on which to build a modern Islamic society presents us with a case similar to the issue facing a growing and modernizing China. There is currently a struggle within various Islamic countries, among religious leaders, and the youthful student populations to define a just society that will both honor Islam and project them into the 21st century. If Allah is on our side why are we not more advanced? The world of Islam is in ferment. Muslim countries are experiencing life after what many see as the failures of nationalism and socialism. Many are searching for a definition of citizenship.[44] This includes those who have left Islam.

This struggle is demonstrated by the impact of the life and writings of a Sudanese mystic named Mahmoud Muhammad Taha. In the years after Sudan became independent, in1956, the role of Islam in the state was

---

[44] See http://www.centerforinquiry.net/isis/islamic_viewpoints/new_ secularism_in_the_arab_world/, accessed 3/11/12.

debated between various groups. Sufists, secular Marxists, and the Muslim Brotherhood all offered their visions. Taha gave a lecture entitled, "An Islamic Constitution: Yes and No." Taha called for a reformed constitution that reconciled the individual need for freedom with the community's need for social justice. A young Muslim boy attended and it changed his life and gave him a profound sense of peace:

> I am a Muslim but I couldn't accept Sharia – Islamic law. I studied Sharia and I knew what it said. I couldn't see how Sudan could be viable without women being full citizens and without non-Muslims being full citizens. I'm a Muslim but I couldn't live with this view of Islam. [45]

A similar story is told of a young Muslim girl just eighteen years old who felt that Muslim custom and law made her a second class citizen. She could not accept that her Muslim faith demanded the death of non-Muslims who refused to convert. She found Taha's book *The Koran, Mustapha Mahmoud, and Modern Understanding* which was published in 1970. When she finished it she was weeping. "Inside this thinking I'm a human being. Outside this thinking I'm not."[46]

---

[45] This and the following anecdote are from George Packer, "Letter from Sudan: The Moderate Martyr," *The New Yorker* (September 1, 2006):p. 61.

[46] Ibid.

Another example of an Islamic author having impact in the Islamic world today is Fahmy Howeidy, an Egyptian lawyer whose book *Citizens, not Dhimmis* argues that Christians in an Islamic state are citizens with rights and duties equal to those of their fellow Muslims. Professor Abdullahi An-Na'im is modernist writer who states that the concept of citizen in Islamic states should be based upon more modern territorial concepts rather than the premodern personal norms.[47]

In order to bind together a contemporary functioning society of such disparate members China must begin to bring these groups into dialog and create a citizenship which all have a stake in protecting. Almost all these social virtues have counterparts in Christian belief and practice. The foundation and source for believing and practicing them are from different conceptions of reality – with each other and with Christianity. But if "citizenship" is to mean anything there must be understanding and respect and a willingness to allow others to have and practice a different world view.

VIII. Non-Christian Epistemology

---

[47] See the internet article "Islamic Citizenship Revisited" for an extended discussion. www.headheeb.blogmosis.com/archives/016456.html Posted Oct. 2, 2003. Accessed 4/25/07.

If China is to become contemporary in the philosophical sense as well as the material sense it should not copy the West. It must reject the despair of postmodernism – defined as a loss of ever finding certainty through reason, science or philosophy. While science and reason have created wonders like flush toilets and refrigeration, it has not solved those pesky age old metaphysical questions that still haunt mankind across time and across the planet. Now we realize and admit that it does appear that all human thought is ultimately based upon assumptions, axioms – in a word, on faith!

Today, many in the West have laughingly discarded religion and metaphysics as a source for answers to truth and value questions. Reality is not clearly defined today as it was thought it would be through the use of reason and science. In the East too some thought religion was an "opiate of the people" that could be educated out of the masses for their own good. But the haunting questions of meaning, purpose, and truth continue to appear in the minds of men.[48]

In the West what has been termed the Age of Reason, or the Enlightenment, arose under the banner of unbiased

---

[48] For an important survey of recent revolutionary faith see: James H. Billington, *Fire in the Minds of Men: Origins of the Revolutionary Faith*, The author looks at the lives of key revolutionaries who converted social theory into political practice during the late eighteenth to the early twentieth centuries.

truth. Man by the careful use of his enlightened reason would throw off the prejudices of the masses (Christianity) and see reality clearly enough to build a state, based upon man's reason, which would lead to a better man and a better world. The Marquis de Condorcet (1743-1794) in his "Sketch for an Historical Picture of the Progress of the Human Mind" stated that mankind had:

> . . ., at last found a sure method of discovering and recognizing truth; and how at the same time it destroyed the prejudices of the masses which had for so long afflicted and corrupted the human race.[49]

Condorcet goes on to say:

> At last man could proclaim aloud his right, which for so long had been ignored, to submit all opinions to his own reason and to use in the search for the truth the only instrument for its recognition that he has been given.[50]

One of the important contemporary critics of the Enlightenment was Johann Georg Hamann (1730-1788). He was a pious Lutheran who wrote against Enlightenment assumptions. He wisely used some sources of the Enlightenment to highlight his arguments. Hamann

---

[49] Cited in Tim Morris and Don Petcher, *Science and Grace: God's Reign in the Natural Sciences*, (Wheaton, IL: Crossway Books, 2006), p.26.

[50] Ibid, p.26.

used Enlightenment skepticism to point out that all foundation of knowledge is based on faith of some kind. For instance, he quoted Hume (1711-1776) speaking against the skeptics writing in his *Treatise on Human Understanding*:

> Thus the skeptic still continues to reason and believe, even tho' he asserts that he cannot defend his reason by reason; and by the same rule he must assent to the principle concerning the existence of body, tho' he cannot pretend by any arguments of philosophy to maintain its veracity . . . We may well ask, *What causes induce us to believe in the existence of body?* But 'tis in vain to ask, *Whether there be body or not?* This is a point, which we must take for granted in all our reasonings.[51]

Isaiah Berlin's (1909-1997) comments on the work of Hamann are worth setting out in some detail:

> . . . our most famous philosophers cut away the branch on which they are sitting, hide like Adam, their unavoidable and agreeable sin; they deny the brute fact, the irrational. Things are as they are; without accepting this there is no knowledge, for all knowledge reposes on belief or faith, . . .

---

[51] David Hume, *Treatise on Human Understanding*, (Oxford: Clarendon Press, 1973), p.187. David. Hume here gives a role to accepting the external world and our own existence without any rational proof. See also, Isaiah Berlin, *Three Critics of the Enlightenment, Vico, Hamann, Herder*, ed., Henry Hardy, (Princeton: Princeton University Press, 2000), p.280, more information on the life and thought of these men.

faith in the existence whether of chairs and tables and trees, or of God and the truth of his Bible, all given to faith, to belief, to no other faculty. The contrast here between faith and reason is for him a profound fallacy. There are no ages of faith followed by ages of reason. These are fictions Reason is built on faith, it cannot replace it; there are no ages that are not ages of both; the contrast is unreal. Irrational religion is a contradiction in terms. A religion is true not because it is rational but because it is face-to-face with what is real; modern philosophers pursue rationality like Don Quizote, and will in the end, like him, lose their wit.[52]

There have been developments in both philosophy and science that have challenged the above skeptical views. Think Postmodernism and Quantum Physics. How can one be absolutely sure of observations, measurements, or theories? "Subjective judgment calls are therefore needed to make decisions as to what is to be trusted. Thus science depends upon prior theoretical commitments in many ways."[53]

It must be admitted and recognized that presuppositions are central to all human thought. A naturalistic worldview (reality is simply physical) proclaims a closed world system of basically mechanistic

[52] Isaiah Berlin, *Three Critics of the Enlightenment*, p.283.

[53] Ibid. p.43.

laws or regularities. Even God, if he exists, is viewed to be subject to these laws. Scholarship, scientific or religious, then follows a project of explaining away the miraculous as impossible or myth. Any revelation from outside of the mind of man of a religious nature is seen in this light. This applies to all religions that claim to have revelation from God. In Western rationalism this applies especially to the Christian Scripture (the Old and New Testaments):

> And if naturalism is true, the traditional picture of the New Testament as the product of divine revelation must also go out the window so that creative scholarship can entertain itself exploring interpretations of 'revelation' that are consistent with its naturalism.[54]

In China the impact of the Western conviction that reason and science was freeing men from religious myths was seen during the May Fourth Movement of 1919 and the Anti-Christian Movement of the 1920s among Chinese intellectuals. As well as viewing Christianity as superstition, there was also the feeling that it was part of Western cultural imperialism. Now however, Christianity may be seen as having taken root on its own in China and no longer under the control of foreign interests. Nestorian Christians traveling along the Silk Road carried

[54] Ronald H. Nash, *The Gospel and the Greeks: Did the New Testament Borrow From Pagan Thought?*. 2nd, ed., (Phillipsburg, NJ: P & R Publishing, 1992), p.249.

Christianity deep into Asia in the early centuries after the time of Christ. Chinese travelers to the East reached as far as Antioch, a center of Christianity, during the early centuries.[55]

It must be recognized that Christianity is not really a "Western" religion, having arisen from the Middle East and then planted in the West at a later time. The study of Christianity requires knowledge of this Middle Eastern thought world to understand its Scriptures.

The truth of the words of Jesus "A man's life does not consist in the abundance of his possessions" [56] were demonstrated once again by the wars and killings of the 20th century. The vision of autonomous man alone in the universe was shown to be thin gruel indeed.

The postmodern epistemological dilemma has been present in one form or another throughout the history of philosophy and religion. Thinkers in all ages have recognized the problem of knowing how men know and if knowledge can ever be certain:

[55] See especially, Rene Grousset, *The Empires of the Steppes: A History of Central Asia*, trans. by Naomi Walford, (New Brunswick, NJ: Rutgers University Press, 2002). and Philip Jenkins, *The Lost History of Christianity: The Thousand-Year Golden Age of the Church in the Middle East, Africa, and Asia – How It Died*, (NY: HarperCollins Publishers, 2008).

[56] Luke 12:15

Dr. Kenneth Arndt

Only one thing is certain – that is, nothing is
certain. If this statement is true, it is also false.
Ancient paradox

We know nothing in reality; for truth lies in an abyss.
Democritus, (c. 420-c, 480 BC)

But as for certain truth, no man has known it,
Nor will he know it; neither of the gods,
Nor yet of all the things of which I speak
And even if by chance he were to utter
The final truth, he would himself not know it;
For all is but a woven web of guesses.
Xenophanes (c. 570-c. 480 BC)

None of us knows anything, not even whether we
know or do not know, nor do we know whether
not knowing and knowing exist, nor in general
whether there is anything or not. *Metrodorus of
Chios,* (c. 4th Century BC)

This only is certain, that there is nothing certain;
and nothing more miserable and yet more
arrogant than man. *Pliny ("The Elder," 35-
79AD)*

All we know of truth is that absolute truth, such
as it is, is beyond our reach. *Nicholas of Cusa,*
(1401-64 AD)

Western philosophy/science, in its search for truth
and meaning, has been built upon the method of doubt put
forward by Descartes' project of skepticism toward any

claim of knowledge. We now, in the postmodern world, realize that "The acids of doubt that Descartes dredged up turned out to be corrosive solvents of every system erected to replace traditional (Christian) sources of knowledge."[57]

Some seek solace and understanding in the pursuit of science as if to find certainty in the workings of nature. Del Ratzsch has said, "We must be cautious about understanding nature's capabilities. During its history science has been surprised by nature pretty regularly, and it may happen again."[58] A case in point is the recent change in the ideas of Anthony Flew (1923-2010) who believed in the possibility of a mind of some kind behind the physical world. In his book *There Is a God: How the World's Most Notorious Atheist Changed His Mind*, he states that because of science he can no longer believe in a purely physical explanation for the beginning of the first replicating life form. His fellow atheists became hysterical in their attacks against him. Here was a man who for fifty years gave a comprehensive and systematic defense of atheism who has now changed his mind – because of science he says! Not a religious conversion, but a change of mind.[59]

---

[57] Vinoth Ramachandra, *Gods That Fail,*. p. 177.

[58] Del Ratzsch, *Science and Its Limits: The Natural Sciences in Christian Perspective* (Downers Grove, IL: InterVarsity Press, 2000), p.132.

[59] Anthony Flew, *There Is a God: How the World's Most Notorious Atheist*

Imre Lakatos (1922-1974) presented in his writings the complicated process by which science is developed.[60] He made the logical point that "One can today easily demonstrate that there can be no valid derivation of a law of nature from any finite number of facts; but we still keep reading about scientific theories being proven from facts."[61] It must also be kept in mind that the "facts"/data which are the result of scientific research require interpretation in all cases.

Philosophical materialism (all reality is material) separates scientific truth from religious or metaphysical truth by claiming that scientific truth is superior to all other forms of truth. Paul Feyerabend (1924-1994) saw science itself as a form of religion:

> Thus science is much closer to myth than a scientific philosophy is prepared to admit. It is one of many forms of thought that have been developed by man, and not necessarily the best. It is conspicuous, noisy, and impudent, but it is inherently superior only for those who have already decided in favor of a certain ideology, or

---

Changed His Mind, with Roy Abraham Varghese, (NY: HarperCollins Publishers, 2007).

[60] See especially his *Proofs and Refutations* (1976) and *The Methodology of Scientific Research Programmes* (1978), both published posthumously.

[61] Imre Lakatos, *The Methodology of Scientific Research Programmes,* Vol.1, p.2.

who have accepted it without having examined its advantages and its limits.[62]

The American professor of physics Donald E. Simanek makes a clear statement as to the thinking today about the limits of science and in particular mathematics:

> Mathematics is a process of deductive logic. Therefore it is ideally suited to be the language and the deductive link between theories and experimental facts. Because of this, some non-scientists think that mathematics and logic are used to "prove" scientific propositions, to deduce new laws and theories, and to establish laws and theories with mathematical certainty. This is false, as we shall see.[63]

The Greeks, starting perhaps with Aristotle, used logic to deduce consequences from premises. The problem men have discovered is that one cannot get more out of the premise than is already there from its definition. As Simanek states, "His error was his failure to realize that we have no absolutely true premises, except ones we *define* to be true (such as 2+2=4)."[64] He goes on to say:

Another error was to assume that the conclusions

---

[62] Paul Feyerabend, *Against Method : Outline of an Anarchistic Theory of Knowledge*, (London, Verso: 1978), p.295.

[63] Quoted in, www.1hup.edu/~dsimanek/logic.htm, accessed 4/28/04.

[64] Ibid.

from a logical argument represent new truths. In fact, the deduced conclusions are just restatements and repackaging of the content contained in the premises. The conclusions may look new to us, because we hadn't thought through the logic, but they contain no more than the information contained in the premises. They are just cast in a new form, a form which may seem to give us new insight and suggest new applications, but in fact no new information or truths are generated. This is especially noticeable in mathematics, for without considerable instruction in mathematics, the deductions from even a small set of premises are not at all obvious, and may take years to develop and understand . . . It must be admitted at the outset that science is not in the business of finding absolute truths. Science proceeds as if there are no absolute truths, or if there are such truths, we can never know what they are. As the pre-Socratic skeptics observed: If we were to stumble upon an absolute truth, we'd have no way to be certain it is an absolute truth. The models and theories of science are approximations to nature – never perfect.[65]

Bertrand Russell (1872-1970) stated in 1951, "all mathematical proof consists merely in saying in other words part or the whole of what is said in the premises."[66]

---

[65] Ibid.

[66] Cited in Stanley Jaki, *Cosmos and Creator*, (Chicago, IL: Regnery Gateway, Inc., 1980), p.158, note 28.

He stated that he began to suspect the tautological basis of mathematics after reading Wittgenstein's *Tractatus*. In 1968 he wrote "I felt a violent repulsion to the suggestion that 'all mathematics is tautology' . . . I came to believe this but I did not like it. I thought mathematics was a splendid edifice, but this shows that it was built on sand."[67]

It becomes apparent to postmodern man that if all truth is relative or that everything is merely a matter of personal opinion then the idea of truth itself loses its significance. We lose the ability to understand the difference between truth and falsehood or sense and nonsense. Here Feyerabend makes the claim that for finite beings with finite data, faith, assumptions, axioms, are the necessary starting place for thought about reality:

> We find then, that there is not a single rule, however plausible, and however firmly grounded in epistemology, that is not violated at some time or other. It becomes evident that such violations are not accidental events, they are not results of insufficient knowledge or of inattention which might have been avoided. On the contrary, we see that they are necessary for progress.[68]

The advances in theoretical mathematics have left

---

[67] Ibid., p. 158, note 28.

[68] Feyerabend, *Against Method*, Vol.1, p.23.

men without a firm foundation for that seemingly most certain of all human endeavors. What could be more certain than that two plus two equals four? But the mathematicians continue to tell us otherwise. Douglas Hofstadter an American scientist (b. 1945) who won the Pulitzer Prize for his important book, *Gödel, Escher, Bach,* describes the state of current mathematical thinking:

> All the limitative Theorems of metamathematics and the theory of computation suggest that once the ability to represent your own structure has reached a certain critical point, that it is the kiss of death: it guarantees that you can never represent yourself totally. Godel's Incompleteness Theorem, Church's Undecidability Theorem, Turing's Halting Theorem, Tarkski's Truth Theorem – all have the flavor of some ancient fairy tale which warns you that, 'To seek self-knowledge is to embark on a journey which... will always be incomplete, cannot be charted on any map, will never halt, cannot be described.' Just as we cannot see our own faces with our own eyes, is it not reasonable to expect that we cannot mirror our own complete mental structures in the symbols which carry them out? [69]

These limits to knowledge for a finite man, with a finite mind and finite data are pointed out by thinkers all the time. Thinking for such a being as man appears to

---

[69] Douglas R. Hofstadter, *Godel, Escher, Bach: An Eternal Braid* (NY: Basic Books, 1979), p.697.

have to start from assumptions, axioms – faith. This it seems impossible to doubt except upon the assertion of other ultimately unprovable claims to truth. This is a fundamental error of what is called *foundationalism* in philosophy. Foundationalism in several versions claims that there is a body of truth that is indisputable or self-validating, or of great probability. However, the Cartesian project of truth arrived at by means of doubt turns out to have limits as well:

> It is logically impossible to doubt all one's ideas at the same time. Whenever we doubt a truth-claim, it is on the basis of other truth-claims which, at that moment, we do not doubt. For instance, the insight that Descartes regarded as basic – the reality of the thinking "I" – is not basic at all. We should have no concept of the self at all if we did not think of it as part of a world of others. [70]

Morris Kline (d.1992) a professor of mathematics at New York University in his multi-volume work, *Mathematical Thought From Ancient To Modern Times,* states:

> Whether or not the optimism is warranted, the

---

[70] Ramachandra, *Gods That Fail*, p.177-178. The later Wittgenstein pointed out that language presupposes a society. The language of self-knowledge makes sense only because it presupposes the existence of others. Just so Christians accept the idea of God as Trinity. The ground of all being as personal presupposes He is more than "One."

present state of mathematics has been aptly described by Weyl: 'The question of the ultimate foundations and the ultimate meaning of mathematics remains open; we do not know in what direction it will find its final solution or even whether a final objective answer can be expected at all. 'Mathematizing' may well be a creative activity of man, like language or music, of primary originality, whose historical decisions defy complete objective rationalization.'[71]

Philosophy as a general discipline:

...as any other reasonable human activity, must be logical, that is, consistent enterprise. But if philosophy is logical by emphasis, it is no longer that love of wisdom which philosophy is by hallowed appellation. Whatever the wisdom of logic (professional logicians, to say nothing of students of logic, rarely give the impression of being men of wisdom), logic operates within its self-imposed conceptual circle and is very different from that love the aim of which is to reach a reality distinct from the self."[72]

The physical sciences are in no better shape concerning certainty. Nigel Brush in his book, *The Limits of Scientific Truth,* writes:

---

[71] Morris Kline, *Mathematical Thought From Ancient To Modern Times* Vol. 3, (NY: Oxford University Press, 1972), p.1210.

[72] Stanley Jaki, *Cosmos and Creator*, p.89.

At the quantum level the fundamental dichotomies between matter and energy, cause and effect, and the observer and the observed all broke down; the walls between subjectivity and objectivity seemed to collapse. Thus, scientists, instead of finding solid bedrock underlying the physical universe, seem to have fallen into a quicksand of subjectivism and illusion. [73]

Scientists of the philosophical materialistic kind seek to understand and explain the question of the *why* of the existence of matter, mind, and human will only in terms of physical processes. But science is itself always and only a project of measurement of the interaction between matter and energy – and that never with absolute exactness. [74] Science never addresses, indeed cannot address purely by measurements, the great *why* questions.

While Scripture teaches that man was created as a finite creature and will always be a creature and finite, by his sin he has become separated from God the absolute reference point. But God has made a way back into fellowship with himself through the cross of Christ. "When you were dead in your sins and in the uncircumcision of your sinful Nature, God made you alive

---

[73] Nigel Brush, *The Limits of Scientific Truth*, (Grand Rapids, MI: Kregel, 2005), p.163.

[74] Modern quantum mechanics permits only the calculation of averages and never exact measurement of individual interactions.

with Christ."[75]

This is the metanarrative of the Gospel - the law and grace. Since being cast out of Eden, all human reasoning of spiritually dead men is at root circular. Postmodern men like all men without spiritual life in God are like Bertrand Russell, locked into a self-culture of ultimate meaningless. "The Christian sense of self- culture is altogether different from the worldly and Christless sense. Nay, in this point to my mind all questions concentrate . . . The question is, Man without God, or Man and God in God"[76]

Either the universe is self-created to no discernible purpose or there is a Creator. Bertrand Russell a British philosopher and mathematician concluded that life must be built within unyielding despair. He gives a horrifying description of the lost soul that should be laid along side of a scriptural picture of hell. Russell who after twenty years of research gave up in despair after looking for certainty in mathematics (set theory) says:

> Man is the product of causes which had no prevision of the end they were achieving; that his origin, his growth, his hopes and fears, his loves and his beliefs, are but the outcome of accidental

---

[75] Colossians 2: 13

[76] Gavin Carlyle, *Mighty in the Scriptures: A Memoir of Adolph Saphir* (Choteau, MT: Old Paths Gospel Press, nd), p.113. The quote is from Adolph Saphir.

collections of atoms; that no fire, no heroism, no intensity of thought and feeling, can preserve an individual life beyond the grave; that all the labor of the ages, all the devotion, all the noonday brightness of human genius, are destined to extinction in the vast death of the solar system, and that the whole temple of man's achievement must inevitably be buried beneath the debris of a universe in ruins -- all these things, if not quite beyond dispute, are yet so nearly certain, that no philosophy which rejects them can hope to stand. Only within the scaffolding of these truths, only on the firm foundation of unyielding despair, can the soul's habitation henceforth be safely built.[77]

Is despair, gazing into the abyss, the fate or longing of mankind? The Good News of the Gospel of Jesus Christ denies that idea. It offers salvation from such a fate. Even an atheist like Bertrand Russell quoted above could not accept his own conclusions. In 1950 Russell stated at Columbia University that was most needed was Christian love. "If you have Christian love you have a motive for existence, a guide for action, a reason for courage, an imperative necessity for intellectual honesty."[78]

Stanley Jaki comments on this stunning admission:

---

[77] Quoted in James Nickel, *Mathematics: Is God Silent?* (Vallecito, CA: Ross House Books, 1990), p.64.

[78] Quoted in Stanly Jaki, *The Only Chaos and Other Essays*, p.264.

Hunger for true love – heroic, self-sacrificing love – remains mankind's basic hunger. Acknowledgment of this comes on occasion even from those who earned their fame (often their fortunes, too) by preaching salvation through science. When Bertrand Russell stated at Columbia University in 1950 that Christian love was the *thing* most needed by modern man, he moved revealingly close to declaring the intellectual bankruptcy on his and many others' behalf. He said much more about Christian love. Although fully familiar with the enormous power of modern science, medicine, and technology he held high Christian love and the *answer* to man's needs in the broadest sense. [79]

James H. Billington responding to the terror as practiced by the revolutions of the twentieth century and their outcomes echoed Russell:

Both Stalin's and Hitler's terrifying reigns were supported by many otherwise educated people. Thus, the mere spread of education throughout the world is hardly a guarantee against the emergence of new forms of violence and repression. Intellectual ingenuity has so far outstripped moral and spiritual development in our time that it is hard to see how the human race will be able to control the awesome powers of destruction that modern science and technology have put in our hands.

---

[79] Ibid. p.264.

I personally believe that the answer to false and
illusory beliefs is not an indefinite suspension of
all belief, but a providential, Christian belief in
responsibility to God and to one's fellow man.
But theology and history both teach us that many
who profess noble beliefs do evil things; and that
many with illusory or no beliefs do good.[80]

Postmodernism states that the very basis of
modernism, the trust in human reason to find certainty and
truth, has failed and it is no longer possible to find truth or
certainty. This is because it is believed that all knowledge
must be based on perspective and subjectivity. All words,
by definition, refer only to other words.

Postmodernism objects to the very idea that there is
any over-arching or absolutely true explanation for man or
for the world as men know it. There is no Big Picture.[81]
What are referred to as metanarratives are seen as
misguided in principle. Metanarrative is used as a word
for metaphysics. Jean Francois Lyotard defines
postmodernism in his book *The Postmodern Condition* as

---

[80] Billington, p.x. He also states: "The present author is inclined to believe
that the end may be approaching of the political religion which saw in
revolution the sunrise of a perfect society. I am further disposed to wonder if
this secular creed, which arose in Judaeo-Christian culture, might not
ultimately prove to be only a stage in the continuing metamorphosis of older
forms of faith and to speculate that belief in secular revolution, which has
legitimized so much authoritarianism in the twentieth century, might
dialectically prefigure rediscovery of religious evolution to revalidate
democracy in the twenty-first." p.14.

[81] One might ask if the this Postmodern statement is itself a "metanarrative?"

"a sense of incredulity toward religious answers."[82] Put another way, there are no absolutes because are there none any man could ever discover. Postmodern non-Christians scoff at the believer's view that there is a loving God who has spoken and cares for his children.

If finite man using the project of science based on the use of reason and experience cannot find an absolute truth what is to be done? Must the scientist become a cynic lost forever in a sea of relativism? Most searchers of truth march on continuing to believe in the scientific method despite its flaws and limitations.

David Hume (1711-1776) struggled with this dilemma of thought stating, "Thus the skeptic still continues to reason and believe, even though he asserts, that he cannot defend his reason with reason."[83] Hume's empiricism had led to the realization that scientific truth cannot be the same as absolute truth. This is because all scientific hypotheses are founded on the use of induction and they can never be proven on the basis of empirical observation. Bertrand Russell responded to Hume's

---

[82] Jean-Francois Lyotard, *The Postmodern Condition* (Manchester University Press, 1984), p.34.

[83] David Hume, *A Treatise of Human Nature*, p.187. Brian Magee has observed, "That the whole of science, of all things should rest on foundations whose validity it is impossible to demonstrate has been found uniquely embarrassing." *Philosophy and the Real World: An Introduction to Karl Popper*, (LaSalle, Ill.: Open Court, 1985), p.17.

problem:

> It is therefore important to discover whether
> there is any answer to Hume within the
> framework of a philosophy that is wholly or
> mainly empirical. If not, there is no intellectual
> difference between sanity and insanity. The
> lunatic who believes he is a poached egg is to be
> condemned solely on the ground that he is in a
> minority, or rather – since we must not assume
> democracy – on the ground that the government
> does not agree with him. It is a desperate point
> of view, and it must be hoped that there is some
> way of escaping from it.[84]

IX. The Christian Basis for Faith – Its Epistemology

Anselm of Canterbury in the Middle Ages coined the
phrase "I believe so that I may understand." When
understood to mean that one does not believe because one
relies on reason first, it is correct. Indeed, postmodern
philosophy and science also begin first with "faith"
statements.

Postmodernism has done away with the
Enlightenment view of autonomous man finding truth
through his own efforts. It has given up the search for or

---

[84] Bertrand Russell, *A History of Western Philosophy* (NY: Simon and Schuster, 1945), p.673.

belief in "infallible beliefs" or "necessary beliefs." In this position postmodern man is at the point of the truth of the scripture which portrays him as unable to understand spiritual things and not in connected to or in communication with the living God. [85] The Christian Scriptures explain how man came to be spiritually dead and unconnected with an infinite reference point from which to obtain meaning and significance:

> In the beginning God created the heavens and the earth . . . Then God said, 'Let us make man in our image' . . . And the Lord God formed man from the dust of the ground and breathed into his nostrils the breath of life, and man became a living being. Now the Lord God had planted a garden in the east, in Eden; and there he put the man he had formed. 'You are free to eat from any tree in the garden; but you must not eat from the tree of the knowledge of good and evil, for when you eat of it you will surely die.' When the woman saw that the fruit of the tree was good for food and pleasing to the eye, and also desirable for gaining wisdom, she took some and ate it. She also gave some to her husband, who was with her, and he ate it. So the Lord God

---

[85] 1 Corinthians 2:14, "The man without the Spirit does not accept the things of God, for they are foolishness to him, and he cannot understand them, because they are spiritually discerned." See also Ezekiel 11:19 "I will give them an undivided heart and put a new spirit in them; I will remove from them their heart of stone and give them a heart of flesh." 2 Corinthians 3:3 "You show that you are a letter from Christ, the result of our ministry, written not with ink but with the Spirit of the living God, not on tablets of stone but on tablets of human hearts."

banished him from the Garden of Eden to work the ground from which he had been taken. After he drove the man out, he placed on the east side of the Garden of Eden cherubim with a flaming sword flashing back and forth to guard the way to the tree of life. [86]

And so mankind was deprived of spiritual life and the ability to "walk with God" and driven out from the presence of God who alone is the source of all meaning and ever after forced to wander as rebels with darkened minds among the continued lies of the Evil One. But God in his mercy has chosen a people for himself - the Sons, the elect - who are to be "born again" to new spiritual life in Christ and for whom the heavens are not brass. For Christians the epistemological problem is solved by the indwelling Spirit. "Born Again" is a term Jesus used. [87] Christians believe the Gospel is true by faith and because of the witness of the God's Holy Spirit given to us at new spiritual birth:

> For you did not receive the spirit of slavery to fall back into fear, but you have received the adoption as sons, by whom we cry, 'Abba! Father!' *The Spirit himself bears witness with our spirit* that we are the children of God and if children, then heirs – heirs of God and fellow

---

[86] Selected passages from Genesis chapters 1-3.

[87] John 3: 3. "Jesus answered him, 'Truly, truly, I say unto you, unless one is born again he cannot see the kingdom of God.'"

heirs with Christ, provided we suffer with him in order that we may also be glorified with him.[88]

St. Paul reminds the Church in Corinth that their faith did not come from the power of his explanation of the Gospel, but from God:

> . . . and my speech and my message were not in plausible words of wisdom, but in demonstration of the Spirit and of power, that your faith might not rest in the wisdom of men, but in the power of God.[89]

Postmodern man stumbles because he cannot, starting from himself, with language or logic formulate or articulate certain knowledge. Even in the Garden of Eden language was apparently not absolute between God and man. Man was pronounced "good" and "very good," but finite. And the Lord Jesus reminds us that only the Father knows the Son and only the Son knows the Father. Only within the Trinity is there absolute communication.

"Fallen" man seeks a way back into the Garden of Eden, as it were, seeking a sure foundation for meaning to life. The Enlightenment Project has proven to be a false

---

[88] Romans 8: 15-17 Note: Italics added. To be "glorified with him" imparts the substance of the word "glory." In Hebrew it carries signifies "heaviness," "meaning," "purpose." In other words, in eternity! See also Luke 12:12 "for the Holy Spirit will teach you . . ., "

[89] I Corinthians 2: 4-5

hope. David Wells sees the postmodern era as a return to a time before the Enlightenment dream of certainty through reason:

> I would scarcely dispute the assertion that we are in the midst of a cultural disjunction, a rending of the fabric of consensual meaning, and a deep and radical displacement of the values, norms, and expectations that have been in place for a long time in America. But I am inclined to think that post-modernity is really just modernity stripped of the false hopes that were once supported by the straw pillars of Enlightenment ideology, the illusions that once rendered modernity at least tolerable for many people. Their faith in the idea of progress proved to be the last Western superstition, and now it has died.[90]

History, while not actually repeating itself, often rhymes. The world recognizes again human finiteness. Mankind is still subject to the limits of the mind, human nature, and the natural world. So science marches on with seemingly no one at the helm, into an uncertain and perhaps grotesque future. How different from the Christian view as expressed by John Calvin a French theologian (1509-1564) who saw God at the helm of the universe. Men in their thinking about the meaning of reality have always reached into the metaphysical realm

---

[90] David F. Wells, *God in the Wasteland: The Reality of Truth In A World of Fading Dreams* (Grand Rapids, MI: InterVarsity Press, 1994), p.216.

for answers to basic questions.[91]

Christians do not demand or expect to attain certain knowledge except by faith in what God has revealed – the same way all knowledge is apparently grasped by finite man. It is understood more than that is beyond our understanding. Calvin, in his *Sermons on the Epistle to the Ephesians* puts the Christian position so well:

> There was not, then, any certain knowledge until God had displayed in effect that which he had kept in his own counsel. And in fact, St. Paul thought it good to repeat the word 'mystery', in order that one man should not provoke another to be more opinionated than we are accustomed to be. For if something is hard, one will say, This is beyond my comprehension, and another makes nothing at all of it. And by that means men turn away from obeying God, and cast as it were, a

---

[91] "From humanity's earliest records human beings have questioned their place in the universe and their relation to some transcendent reality. Those questions took exquisite intellectual form in the writings of the Greek philosophers, among whom Plato and Aristotle were preeminent teachers. Although individual philosophers developed a variety of systems to envision the structure of their universe, common to all Greek thought was a dualism that separated the material and non-material worlds into two distinct categories. Human beings live in a material world but they are equipped with sufficient imagination to conceive of a non-material, spiritual realm, that, because of their carnality, they cannot know by direct participation." Quoted in Parker T. Williamson, *Standing Firm: Reclaiming Christian Faith in Times of Controversy* (Lenior, NC: PLC Publications, 1996), p.37.

stumbling block in people's ways, so that their way and passage is stopped up, and none come near God's truth . . .Therefore, let us learn to magnify God's wisdom, for though his counsel may be obscure to us, yet we may not therefore reject it, but honor it with all humility . . . And there are other matters, in which God reserves the reasons to himself, meaning thereby to hold us in check, to make us confess that all his doings are just, although we cannot agree to it with our own natural understanding, or conceive in our mind the reason why it should be so.[92]

X. A Distinctly Christian Model of Citizenship

All societies, indeed all persons attempting to make sense of reality and form an articulate worldview address some basic questions:

- What am I?

- Who am I'

- Where did I come from?

- Where am I going?

- What is my purpose?

---

[92] John Calvin, *Sermons on the Epistle to the Ephesians* (Carlisle, PA: The Banner of Truth Trust, 1987), p.236.

The contemporary world seems to have answered these questions this way:

- We are Chimps (Evolution/"goo to you"/no purpose/no "soul")

- We are Chemicals (above plus materially determined mind and body)

- We are Computers (above plus simply electro/mechanical beings)

- We are Created (A religious answer - more than just material beings)

The Christian answer (that we are created) responds to the basic questions:

- Where did we come from? "In the beginning God created the heavens and the earth." (Genesis 1:1)

- Who am I? "So God created man in his own image." (Genesis !:27)

- What is the purpose of life? "Fear God and keep his commandments, for this is the whole duty of man." (Ecclesiastes 12:13b)

- What happens after I die? "And just as man is appointed once to die and after that comes judgment." (Hebrews 9:27)

How different is the current Western experience of man's Church life from that seen in the writings of the early Church Fathers and the testimonies of the pagans. Shielded by great wealth and health the Western churches have grown soft and think they have these benefits as a blessing from God. But perhaps it is not a blessing but a test. Cyprian (190-258 A.D.),[93] the overseer of the church in Carthage, wrote in a letter to a Christian friend:

> The one peaceful and trustworthy tranquility, the one security that is solid, firm, and never changing, is this; for a man to withdraw from the distractions of the world, anchor himself in the firm ground of salvation, and lift his eyes from earth to heaven . . . He who is actually greater than the world can crave nothing, can desire nothing, from this world. How stable, how unshakable is that safeguard, how heavenly is the protection in its never-ending blessings – to be free from the snares of this entangling world, to be purged from the dregs of earth, and fitted for the light of eternal immortality.[94]

---

[93] He was beheaded for his faith.

[94] Quoted in, David W. Bercot, *Will the Real Heretics Please Stand Up: A Look At Today's Evangelical Church In the Light of Early Christianity* (Tyler, TX: Stroll Publishing, 1999), pp.17-18.

A pagan antagonist of the Christians wrote:

> They despise the temples as houses of the dead.
> They reject the gods. They laugh at sacred
> things. Wretched, they pity our priests. Half-
> naked themselves, they despise honors and
> purple robes. What incredible audacity and
> foolishness! They are not afraid of present
> torments, but they fear those that are uncertain
> and future. While they do not fear to die for the
> present, they fear to die after death. See, many of
> you – in fact, by your own admission, the
> majority of you – are in want, are cold, are
> hungry, and are laboring in hard work. Yet, your
> god allows it. [95]

Cyprian also responded to the concerns of some Christians of his day who were attacked by the plague just like the pagans and wondered where God was when they prayed for deliverance:

> It disturbs some that the power of this disease
> attacks our people in the same way it attacks the
> pagans. As if the Christian believed in order to
> have the pleasures of the world and a life free
> from illness, instead of enduring adversity here
> and awaiting a future joy. As long as we are here
> on earth, we experience the same fleshly
> tribulations as the rest of the human race,
> although we are separated in the spirit . . . So
> when the earth is barren with an unproductive

---

[95] Ibid., 18.

harvest, famine makes no distinction. When an invading army captures a city, all are taken as captives alike. When serene clouds withhold rain, the drought is alike to all . . . We have eye diseases, fevers, and feebleness of the limbs the same as others.[96]

In a later age John Calvin taught and preached that we should expect to suffer in his world:

. . . Micah maintains that though we are subject to God and comply with his will, we will still experience travail, that is, we will not be exempt from the tribulations of the world. God will still punish us for our sins and rebellious acts. Nonetheless, in the end, we will see that we deserved such punishment, and that God never allows our travail to be in vain, or useless, or for us to become frustrated during our wait, as is the case when we trust in the world and in ourselves. That is the assurance that Micah gives us, that so long as we are patient under adversity, invoke God, and seek our refuge in him, we need not doubt that we will experience God's help in the midst of our worst afflictions and that God will provide a joyful and happy outcome to all our sufferings.[97]

John Piper tells the story of a young Huguenot girl,

---

[96] Cyprian *On Morality*, section 8, paraphrased in Bercot *Will the Real Heretics Please Stand Up?, p.89.*

[97] John Calvin, *Sermons of the Book of Micah* (Philipsburg, NJ: P & R Publishing, 2003), p.280.

fourteen years old, who was brought before the authorities and required to renounce her faith by simply saying *"j'abjure."* She refused to comply, and together with thirty other women, was confined in a tower by the sea. She continued there for the next thirty-eight years, and instead of *"j'abjure,"* she, with her fellow prisoners, scratched one word on the wall –" *resistez.* "[98]

In the early church, new believers heard a very different message from many in the Western Churches today. Being a Christian would entail suffering. These words of Lactantius (250-325 A.D.) were perhaps typical:

> He who chooses to live well for eternity, will live in discomfort for the present. He will be subjected to all types of troubles and burdens as long as he is on earth, so that in the end he will have divine and heavenly consolation. On the other hand, he who chooses to live well for the present will fare badly in eternity.[99]

---

[98] The story is related in Douglas Wilson, *For Kirk and Covenant: The Stalwart Courage of John Knox* (Nashville, TN: Highland Books, 2000), p.56. One Huguenot on his way to the galleys wrote to his wife: "We lie fifty-three of us in a place which is not about thirty feet in length and nine in breath. . . . There is scarce one of us who does not envy the condition of several dogs and horses. . . . When I reflect on the merciful providence of God towards me, I am ravished with admiration and do evidently discover the secret steps of Providence which hath formed me from my youth after a requisite manner to bear what I suffer," p.48.

[99] Quoted in, David W. Bercot, p.48.

Christians should have a distinct message to describe their vision of how their theology and teaching and living in community the people of God must present themselves to the world. It is the story of God's love for us and our love for others all made possible by the power of God through the work of Christ for us. Sermons and theology are not just rationally worked out philosophical explanations of belief or a defense of doctrine, but a means to create community here and now on the earth:

> The ultimate purpose of theology is not simply to establish right belief but to assist the Christian community in its vocation to *live* as people of God in the particular social-historical context in which they are situated. The goal of theology is to facilitate and enable authentic performance of the Christian faith by the community in its various cultural locations. [100]

This is a very serious business. It is not a lifestyle; it is a new spiritual life. Soren Kierkegaard (1813-1855) [101] the Danish philosopher, railed against a "Culture Christians" church that sees itself on a pleasant stroll to heaven en masse:

---

[100] Kenneth Tanner and Christopher A. Hall editors, *Ancient and Postmodern Christianity: Paleo-Orthodoxy in the 21st Century, Essays in Honor of Thomas C. Oden* . (Downers Grove, IL: InterVarsity Press, 2002), p.238.

[101] At his funeral his brother tried to apologize for his writings but his friends caused a riot over his remarks.

> In the New Testament the Savior of the world, our Lord Jesus Christ, represents the situation thus: The way that leadeth unto life is straitened, the narrow gate – few they be that find it! . . .Now on the contrary, to speak only of Denmark, we are all Christians, the way is as broad as it can possibly be, . . . since the way in which we are all walking, besides being in all respects as convenient, as comfortable, as possible; and the gate as wide as it possibly can be, wider surely than a gate cannot be than that through which we all are going en masse.[102]

Christian sermonizing and life styles need to proclaim a clear statement of what and who defines the church. Kierkegaard insisted that the church must be separate from the world and quotes John 15:18-19:

> If the world hates you, you know that it hated Me before it hated you. If you were of the world, the world would love its own. Yet because you are not of the world, but I chose you out of the world, therefore the world hates you.[103]

---

[102] See his work *Attack Upon Christianity* in which he defines "Christianity" as the national church to which everyone belongs and which, he feels, few take seriously.

[103] Ibid, p.142. "That the Christianity of the New Testament is a thing most repugnant to us men (to the Jews a stumbling block, to the Greeks foolishness), that it is as though calculated to stir us men up against it, that as soon as it is heard it is the signal for the most passionate hate and the cruelest persecution, of this the New Testament makes no concealment; on the contrary it affirms it as

Stanley J. Grenz (1950-2005) an American Evangelical writer states his vision of the impact of Christian belief as follows:

> We believe that the Christian vision, focused as it is on God as the trinity of persons and humankind as created to be the *image dei*, set forth more completely the nature of community that all religious belief systems in their own way and according to their own understanding see to foster. This vision, we maintain provides the best transcendent basis for the human ideal of life-in-relationship, for it looks to the divine life as a plurality-in-unity as the basis for understanding what it means to be human persons-in-community.[104]

From the answers to these questions philosophical, political, or religious, we create our individual lives and our social lives. If the answers are only applied to an individual as an individual that works fine if one is Robinson Crusoe on a island all alone. Only the constraints of Nature bind us. But the moment Crusoe saw in the sand the footprint of another human being, there was

---

distinctly and decisively as possible. It is heard constantly when Christ is talking with the Apostles, saying that they must not be offended; it is emphasized again and again that they must be well prepared for what awaited them.", p.142.

[104] Stanley J. Grenz, "Beyond Foundationalism: Is a Nonfoundationalist Evangelical Theology Possible?" *Christian Scholar's Review* XXX:1 (Fall 2000), p.81.

"society" and the need to create a form of citizenship. We build a concept of "citizen."

The American Protestant model for Christian citizenship has perhaps best been summed up in the work of Carl F. H. Henry (1913-2003) an American theologian who wrote in his books and as editor of the *Christianity Today* magazine about his vision of Christian citizenship:

> Surely Evangelical Christianity has more to offer mankind than its unique message of salvation, even if that is its highest and holiest mission . . . The evangelical knows that spiritual regeneration restores men to moral earnestness but he also knows the moral presuppositions of a virile society, and he is obligated to proclaim the "whole counsel" of God. He may have no message for society that ensures unrepentant mankind against final doom . . . But he can and aught to use every platform of social involvement to promulgate the revealed moral principles that sustain a healthy society . . . [105]

The Christian position must be carefully laid out to the state and fellow non-Christian citizens. There is a stand that Christians take that does not allow them to obey the state when the state authority conflicts with the

---

[105] From Carl F. H. Henry, "Evangelicals in the Social Struggle," *Christianity Today* (8 October 1965): p.6. Quoted in David L. Weeks, "The Uneasy Politics of Modern Evangelicalism," *Christian Scholar's Review* XXX:4 (Summer 2001), p.405.

authority of what God has said. Jesus made this very plain when he said, "Render to Caesar the things that are Caesar's and to God the things that are God's."[106] The Apostles Peter and John when commanded by the authorities to stop speaking about Jesus refused to do so. "But Peter and John answered them, 'Whether it is right in the sight of God to listen to you rather than to God, you must judge."[107]

In 286 A.D. the Theban Legion of the Roman Empire (6,600 men) were almost all Christians. They were ordered by the Emperor Maximian to offer sacrifice to the gods and march to slay the Christians of Gaul. They refused to take the oath and to kill their fellow Christians. Eventually, after killing only some of them, the Emperor had the entire legion executed. Just before this happened they offered the following document to the Emperor as an explanation for their refusal:

> While your commands are not contradictory to those of our common master, we shall always be ready to obey, as we have been hitherto, but when the orders of our prince and those of the Almighty differ, we must always obey the latter. Our arms are devoted to the Emperor's use, and shall be directed against his enemies; but we

---

[106] Mark 12: 17

[107] Acts 4: 19

cannot submit to stain our hands with Christian blood; and how, indeed, could you, O Emperor, be sure of our allegiance and fidelity, should we violate our obligation to our God, in whose service we were solemnly engaged before we entered the army? You command us to search out and to destroy the Christians: it is not necessary to look any farther for people of that denomination; we ourselves are such, and we glory in the name. We saw our companions fall without the least opposition or murmuring and thought them happy in dying for the sake of Christ. Nothing shall make us lift up our hands against our sovereign; we had rather die wrongfully, and by that means preserve our innocence, than live under a load of guilt: whatever you command we are ready to suffer; we confess ourselves to be Christians, and therefore cannot persecute Christians, nor sacrifice to idols. [108]

---

[108] From *The New Encyclopedia of Christian Martyrs* Compiled by Mark Water (Grand Rapids, MI: Baker Books, 2000), pp.346-347.

Conclusion

It must not be supposed that there is one complete and correct model of Christian citizenship. There are general principles to be derived from the Scriptures but from these general principles we are to build for our time and place a work in process that consist of practices that are both faithful to the Christian message and to our calling to be "salt and light" in the world.[109]

An example of these Scriptural principles is seen in the following verses. Here Jesus tells his disciples what the outworking of Christian love should be:

> You have heard that it was said, 'You should love your neighbor and hate your enemy.' But I say to you, Love your enemies and pray for those who persecute you, so that you may be sons of your Father who is in heaven. For he makes the sun to rise on the evil and the good, and sends rain on the just and the unjust. For if you love those who love you, what reward do you have? [110]

---

[109] See Matt. 5: 13-14 Salt and light are used to denote wisdom and knowledge that preserves and radiates God's truth to mankind. "God's word and the prayers of Christians sustain the world." – Martin Luther

[110] Matthew 5: 43-46b

Dr. Kenneth Arndt

Paul in his letter to the Roman Christians outlines what is the proper ethical position and role of a citizen in Roman society:

> Let love be genuine. Abhor what is evil: hold fast to what is good. Love one another with brotherly affection. Outdo one another in showing honor. Do not be slothful in zeal, be fervent in spirit, serve the Lord. Rejoice in hope, be patient in tribulation, be constant in prayer. Contribute to the needs of the saints and seek to show hospitality.
>
> Bless those who persecute you, bless and not curse them. Rejoice with those who rejoice, weep with those who weep. Live in harmony with one another. Do not be haughty, but associate with the lowly. Never be conceited. Repay no one evil for evil, but give thought to do what is honorable in the sight of all. If possible, so far as it depends on you, live peaceably with all. Beloved, never avenge yourselves, but leave it to the wrath of God, for it is written, 'Vengeance is mine, I will repay, says the Lord.' . . . Do not be overcome by evil, but overcome evil with good. [111]

The working out of these general principles and practices are explained by Lawrence L. Adams in his article *Christians and Public Culture in an Age of Ambivalence*:

---

[111] Romans 12: 9-21

Public culture continually demonstrates the need for tangible embodiment of the good life and that abstract statements do not stand alone. So even as they go about their primary task of serving the kingdom of heaven and preparing citizens for it, churches may also cultivate the responsibility and commitment necessary to the formation of temporal public culture. For here in the church is revealed, love for others is demonstrated and cultivated, community is experienced, sacrifice and service and self-denial are practiced. In a fragmentary public culture, a coherent community life may have much more to say than a rationalistic system. Building coherent community is still the most significant public and political responsibility of Christian leadership as we approach the new millennium. Coherent public philosophies will complement this essential task, but serve little in its absence.[112]

While it can be recognized that Christianity came to China from another culture (as did Buddhism and Marxism) the core values of Christianity strike us as having great similarities with traditional Chinese values, especially that of Confucian *xiao*. Taking *xiao* to mean not only filial piety but the obligation of those protected to those who protect and student to teacher. The Hebrew word *kabed* also implies such an idea:

---

[112] Lawrence L. Adams, "Christians and Public Culture in an Age of Ambivalence." *Christian Scholar's Review* XXX:1 (Fall 2000), p36.

You must be *kabed* to your father and your mother, so you live a long time in the land the Lord your God is giving you. (Exodus 20:12) Listen to your father who gave you birth, and don't look down on or despise your mother when she is old . . . Let your father and your mother be glad: and she who bore you celebrate! (Proverbs 23:22, 25) Stand in the presence of a person with grey hair, honor the elderly and revere your God. I am the Lord! (Leviticus 19:32) [113]

The Christian West also has a problem of finding a core set of values upon which to build a foundation of solid and workable citizenship. Judge Robert H. Bork, an American high court judge, sees a revival of religion as the only solution for America. "It thus appears, at least for society as a whole, that the major and perhaps only alternative to intellectual and moral relativism and or nihilism is religious faith."[114]

The very religious faith now rejected by the Western nations (Christianity) had given it the values, however

---

[113] Without stretching the issue too far one might also equate the Confucian concept of *Sheng Ren*, most often translated into English as "Sage" with the Christian doctrine of the Incarnation (Deity) of Christ. The Confucian scholar Chen Jingpan describes the *Sheng Ren* concept thus, "A Sage would have transcended the achievements of any living being which had so far existed. He was thought of as being in the same category as the Divine Being of whom the Superior Man should stand in awe." Chen Jingpan, *Confucius as a Teacher*, (Foreign Languages Press: Beijing, 1990), p.170.

[114] Robert H. Bork, *Slouching Towards Gomorrah: Modern Liberalism and America's Demise.* (NY: HarperCollins, 1996), p.277.

poorly followed, to build a powerful modern world of plenty. Having become rich it has become prideful by seeking to build the Kingdom of Heaven on earth and have instead built a Kingdom of Man. This is the outcome of the sin of Pride. It is the sin of a man trying to be God:

> It is the sin which proclaims that Man can produce out of his own wits and his own impulses and his own imagination the standards by which he lives: that Man is fitted to be his own judge. . . . . The name under which Pride walks the world at this moment is the *Perfectibility of Man*, or the *Doctrine of Progress*; and its specialty is the making of blueprints for Utopia and establishing the Kingdom of Man on earth.[115]

As China enters the 21st century it is not at all certain how it will reinvent itself as communism steps back from the public square and consumerism steps forward to raise the standard of living for many Chinese. The roots of Chinese society in the family system of tradition and the Chinese form of bureaucracy that has held sway for so many years will face challenges from the modern world. If the Party-state suffers from too much lack of public confidence and corruption, and is too rigid so that it cannot adapt fast enough to hold together, then the vision of

---

[115] Dorothy L. Sayers, *Creed or Chaos*, (Manchester, NH: Sophia Institute Press, 1974), p.110.

China as a super-power in the 21st century may fail.[116]

Let us conclude our search for a model of a Chinese Christian citizen in contemporary China with the words of Peter to the early Christians living under the Roman Empire of that time:

> Dear friends, I urge you, as aliens and strangers in the world, to abstain from sinful desires, which war against your soul. Live such good lives among the pagans that, though they accuse you of doing wrong, they may see your good deeds and glorify God on the day he visits us. Submit yourselves for the Lord's sake to every authority instituted among the pagans that, though they accuse you of doing wrong, they may see your good deeds and glorify God on the day he visits us. Submit yourselves for the Lord's sake to every authority instituted among men: whether to the king, as the supreme authority, or to governors, who are sent by him to punish those who do wrong and to commend those who do right. For it is God's will that by doing so you should silence the ignorant talk of foolish men. Live as free men, but do not use your freedom as a cover-up for evil; live as servants of God. Show respect to everyone: Love the brotherhood

---

[116] See "Conclusion: China in the Twenty-First Century" John Bryan Starr, *Understanding China: A Guide to China's Economy, History, and Political Culture.* (NY: Hill and Wang, 2001), pp. 318-323. He feels that near term actions will have large long term implications with no charismatic leader with a program on the horizon.

of believers, fear God, honor the king.[117]

Christians know that their beliefs, their lives, and their service will not always be accepted in a sinful world. They know that honoring God and the state in this way will sometimes involve suffering. But Peter goes on to encourage us:

> But if you suffer for doing good and you endure it, this is commendable before God. To this you were called, because Christ suffered for you, leaving you an example, that you should follow in his steps.[118]

In the contemporary world with all its various forms of government and rapidly developing technologies that allow for the observation and control of populations, states must come to the clear realization that they cannot control, and should not punish, the holding of wrong opinions by

---

[117] 1st Peter 2: 11-17.

[118] 1st Peter 2: 20-21 The Apostle Paul in his letter to Tituis says the same thing: "Remind the people to be subject to rulers and authorities, to be obedient, to be ready to do good, to slander no one, to be peaceablel and considerate, and to show true humility toward all men. At one time we too were foolish, disobedient, deceived and enslaved by all kinds of passions and pleasures. We lived in malice and envy, being hated and hating one another. But when the kindness and love of God our Savior appeared, he saved us, not because of righteous things we had done, but because of his mercy. He saved us through the washing of rebirth and renewal by the Holy Spirit, whom he poured out on us generously throuogh Jesus Christ our Savior, so that having been justified by his grace, we might become heirs having the hope of eternal life." Titus 3:1-7.

members of the populace.[119] It is only when such opinions undermine the well-being of the state that governments may command behavior. Christians are commanded by their Scriptures to be good citizens who contribute to the well-being of their fellow man and the state.

---

[119] Surely a Communist government will recognize the outworking of a dialectic in this process of contending opinions and not fear it.

Final Points

- Christians in each age and culture must, based upon Scriptural principles, define their own model of a Christian Citizen.

- However this model is worked out, it leads to a community dedicated to lives of service and faithfulness to God's Word even in the face of persecution.

- Christian believers are "born again" with new spiritual life and have the witness of God's Holy Spirit that they are his children.

- Science, philosophy, other visions of reality by autonomous man do not have God's revelation of himself and his truth, new birth, or the witness of the Spirit.

- China is at a crossroads as economic liberalization carries with it social liberalization.

- Secular and religious organizations in China all have value concepts of what defines good citizenship.

- There exist overlapping values among these organizations, even if founded upon different principles and beliefs.

- Chinese Christians have their own voice at the national debate as bearers of community values. Perhaps the most important value we offer is love – even to our enemies.

- The fulfillment of the obligation of Chinese Christians to God and the State require that they create and demonstrate a model of Christian citizenship.

- The Chinese Church, like all churches, will move forward by God's power at His timing as witness to the truth of the Gospel.

- All Christians must expect to receive what the Lord has promised us: the honor and ability to serve and to suffer for Him.

- Christian suffering is not something looked for but when it comes it is accepted as having a purpose sent from God or a greater purpose in his Kingdom.

- A harmonious society must, it seems, be centered on an authority higher than the mind of man.

- Christians are not ever perfect in this life. In the words of Martin Luther we are *[simul iustus et peccator*, simultaneously justified and sinful].

- "We do not fundamentally transform the world with our ideas or our principles or our revolutions, but it is the Risen Christ, who bears the new world within himself, who transforms men and women into conformity with himself."[120]

Dr. Kenneth G. Arndt

kgarndt@gmail.com

---

[120] Ramachandra, *Gods That Fail*, p.210.

Dr. Kenneth Arndt

Select Bibliography

Adams, Lawrence E. "Christians and Public Culture in an Age of Ambivalence." *Christian Scholar's Review* XXX 1 (Fall 2000): pp.11-36.

Becker, Jasper. *The Chinese*. NY: The Free Press, 2000.

This volume is a good introduction to the Chinese, their history and culture. It should of course be balanced with other sources.

Bercot, David W. *Will the Real Heretics Please Stand Up: A New Look at Today's Evangelical Church in Light of Early Christianity*. Tyler, TX: Scroll Publishing, 1999.

An interesting and insightful examination of the American (Western) Church today that gives numerous examples of how past generations of Christians have responded to similar challenges.

Billington, James H. *Fire In the Minds of Men: Origins of the Revolutionary Faith*. New Brunswick, NJ: Transaction Publishers, 2007.

James H. Billington is currently the Librarian of Congress and at one time was the director of the Fulbright Program. He is the author of several important historical studies on Russian history.

Bork, Robert H. *Slouching Toward Gomorra: Modern*

Liberalism and America's Decline. NY: HarperCollins, 1996.

Judge Bork points out what happens when a core set of values is lost in a society - in this case American values.

Brush, Nigel. *The Limits of Scientific Truth*. Grand Rapids, MI: Kregel, 2005.

This book is an excellent consideration of the limits of the pursuit of science and has some thought provoking comments and quotes on the issues.

Calvin, John. *Sermons on the Epistle to the Ephesians*. Carlisle, PA: The Banner of Truth Trust, 1987.

------- *Sermons of the Book of Micah*. Philipsburg, NJ: P & R Publishing, 2003.

Calvin's comments and commentary on the Scriptures, though dated, are always insightful and well worth the effort of reading.

Grenz, Stanley J. "Beyond Foundationalism: Is a Nonfoundationalist Evangelical Theology Possible?" *Christian Scholar's Review* XXX 1 (Fall 2000), pp. 57-82.

This is a thoughtful answer to the question. It addresses the epistemological problem as faced by Christians.

Hofstadter, Douglas R. *Godel, Escher, Bach: An Eternal Braid*. NY: Basic Books, 1979.

This is a difficult book to read for the non-scientifically minded. But there are many gems of explanation of the limits of science recognized in the scientific community today.

Jaki, Stanley. *Cosmos and Creator*. Chicago, IL: Regnery Gateway, 1980.

------- *The Only Chaos and Other Essays*. Lanham, MD: University Press of America, Inc., 1990.

Johnson, Paul. *The Renaissance: A Short Story*. London: Phoenix Press, 2000.

Kline, Morris. *Mathematical Thought From Ancient To Modern Times*. Vol. 3, NY: Oxford University Press, 1972.

-------*Mathematics: The Loss of Certainty*. NY: Oxford University Press, 1980.

Kline describes the revolution in mathematics that has led us to a more humble approach to truth approached by science.

Le Carre, John. *Absolute Friends*. Boston: Little & Brown, 2003.

While a novel, this book reflects the culture in the West that no longer has a vision of absolute truth comprehended by man; a vision worth fighting and dying for.

Lopez, Jr., Donald S. ed. *Religions of Asia in Practice*. Princeton: Princeton University Press, 2002.

This work is a good introduction to the religions of Asia and their practices as seen in theory from the West. Of course those living in the East may see reality as different from the theory.

Lyotard, Jean-Francois. *The Postmodern Condition.* Manchester University Press, 1984.

A standard explanation of postmodernism from one of it's leading adherents.

Morris, Tim and Don Petcher. *Science and Grace: God's Reign In the Natural Sciences*, Wheaton, IL: Crossway Books, 2006.

This book is very helpful for sketching out the shift from the Enlightenment to Postmodernism as it has impacted scientific thinking.

Nash, Ronald H. *The Gospel and the Greeks: Did the New Testament Borrow From Pagan Thought?* 2nd ed., Phillipsburg, NJ: P & R Publishing, 2006.

Deals with the question if the early Church borrowed ideas and practices from the surrounding culture of that time. He answers in the negative.

Packer, George, "Letter from Sudan: The Moderate Martyr" *The New Yorker* (September 1, 2006), pp 61-69.

An excellent article that deals in depth with the struggle of values in modern Islamic countries, especially among the young and the intellectuals.

Ramachandra, Vinoth. *Gods That Fail: Modern Idolatry and Christian Mission.* Downers Grove, IL: InterVarsity Press, 1996.

This is an excellent and thought provoking book. See

especially chapter six, "Science and Anti-Science."

Ratzsch, Del. *Science and Its Limits: The Natural Sciences in Christian Perspective.* Downers Grove, IL: InterVarsity, Press, 2000.

As stated in the title this is a good view of modern science and it's limits from a Christian perspective.

Starr, John Bryan. *Understanding China: A Guide to China's Economy, History and Political Culture.* NY: Hill and Wang, 2001.

The author gives a good survey of modern China from the Western viewpoint.

Tanner, Kenneth and Christopher A. Hall, eds. *Ancient and Postmodern Christianity: Paleo-Orthodoxy in the 21st Century, Essays in Honor of Thomas C. Oden.* Downers Grove, IL: InterVarsity Press, 2002.

Valency, Maurice. *The End of the World: An Introduction to Contemporary Drama.* NY: Oxford University Press, 1980.

Valency outlines the current state of the arts as he sees them today in the West.

Walter, Mark. *The New Encyclopedia of Christian Martyrs.* Grand Rapids, MI: Baker Books, 2000.

Weeks, David L. "The Uneasy Politics of Modern Evangelicalism" *Christian Scholar's Review* XXX:4 (Summer 2001), pp.403-418.

Wells, David F. *God in the Wasteland: The Reality of Truth in a World of Fading Dreams.* Grand Rapids, MI: InterVarsity Press, 1994.

This book is a classic among Evangelicals in the West. It responds to the impact of postmodernism upon the Church in the West.

Williamson, Parker T. *Standing Firm: Reclaiming Christian Faith in Times of Controversy.* Lenior, NC: PLC Publications, 1996.

Wilson, Douglas. *For Kirk and Covenant: The Stalwart Courage of John Knox.* Nashville, TN: Highland Books, 2000.

Made in the USA
Charleston, SC
16 July 2014